Life Lessons

Life Lessons

AN INSPIRATIONAL
INSTRUCTION BOOK

Robert C. Savage

INSPIRATIONAL PRESS

New York

LIFE LESSONS: AN INSPIRATIONAL INSTRUCTION BOOK

Copyright © 1993 by Robert C. Savage

Adapted from *Pocket Wisdom* copyright © 1984 and
Pocket Smiles copyright © 1984 by Robert C. Savage

Published in 1993 by Inspirational Press
A division of Budget Book Service, Inc.
386 Park Avenue South, New York, NY 10016

Inspirational Press is a registered trademark of Budget Book Service, Inc.
Published by arrangement with Tyndale House Publishers, Inc.

ISBN: 0-88486-082-5

Designed by Cindy LaBreacht.
Printed in the United States of America.

LIFE LESSONS

The greatest ability is dependability.

You can measure a man by the opposition
it takes to discourage him.

It's easy enough to be pleasant when everything goes
like a song; but the man worthwhile is the man who
can smile when everything goes dead wrong.

1

Avoid following the crowd.
Be an engine—not a caboose.

❧

Those who are willing to face the music,
may some day lead the band.

☙

There's an old saying,
"Erasers are for people who make errors."
A better expression is, "Erasers are for people
who are willing to correct their mistakes!"

Remember the turtle—
he never makes any progress
until he sticks his neck out.

ॐ

The fellow who will never admit he was wrong
really is saying he is no smarter now
than he used to be.

♠

The main difference between the wise man and a fool
is that a fool's mistakes never teach him anything.

I do not think that I should drink.
For when I drink, I do not think.
Isn't it rather foolish for a man to put into his mouth
that which takes away his brains?

Some men—battle to the top;
Others—bottle to the bottom.

Some people think they are big shots
because they are always exploding!

4

The anger of a good man lasts
an instant; that of a meddler,
two hours; that of a base man,
a day and a night; and that of a
great sinner, until death.
(Sanskrit)

The trouble with letting off steam is—
it only gets you into more hot water.

He who blows his stack
adds to the world's pollution.

Some people make a great fuss
over a comet in the sky or a total eclipse,
but never notice a sunset.

An atheist cannot find God for the same reason
a thief cannot find a policeman.

🍃

People who say they sleep like a baby
undoubtably don't have one.

🐚

A driver is the safest when the roads are dry...
but the road is safest when the driver is dry.

Many people, when they run into
a telephone pole, blame the pole!

ﾟﾞ

A bachelor is a man who never made
the same mistake once.

↫

The man who has a right to boast
doesn't have to.

ﾟﾞ

He who is born of God
can and should resemble his Father.

8

Our strength is shown
in the things we stand for;
Our weakness is shown
in the things we fall for.

Reputation is valuable;
but character is priceless.

Much can be analyzed of a man's character
by noting what excites his laughter.

A good way to keep
your feet on the ground
is to put the weight
of responsibilities
on your shoulders.

Men of genius are admired;
men of wealth are envied;
men of power are feared;
but only men of character are trusted.

ੴ

What lies *behind* us or *before* us—
are tiny matters compared with what lies *in us*.

↬

Going to church in the morning is nullified
if you plan to go to the devil in the evening.

11

Now is the best time to do something pleasant
if you want to have pleasant memories.

You are never fully dressed until you wear a smile.

Isn't it wonderful the way youngsters
always brighten up the home?
They never turn out the lights!

The persons hardest to convince
they're at the retirement age are children at bedtime.

A wayward child
is sometimes straightened out
by being bent over.

❧

When adults act like children,
they are silly.
When children act like adults,
they are delinquents.

❦

Striking while the iron is hot is OK,
but don't strike while the head is hot.

Circumstances are like a mattress:
when we are on top, we rest in comfort;
when we are underneath, we are smothered.

❧

Our experts, scientists, researchers and politicians
have gone to a lot of trouble to improve everything
except people.

❦

Blessed is he who will work as a member
of the committee of which he really wanted
to be the chairman.

14

Don't think
you are necessarily
on the right road because
it is a well-beaten path.

The Ten Commandments are short and to the point, so obviously they were not the work of a committee.

ß‍

A bureaucrat's idea of cleaning up his files is to make a copy of every paper before he destroys it.

⊸

Guidelines for bureaucrats:
1) When in charge ponder.
2) When in trouble delegate.
3) When in doubt mumble.

16

Committee—a group of men
who individually can do nothing
but as a group decide
that nothing can be done.

❧

Common sense is just about
the most uncommon thing there is.

❧

Don't grumble because you don't have
what you want...rather be exceedingly grateful
you don't get what you deserve!

17

It is not the greatness of my trials
but the littleness of my faith
that causes me to complain.

✄

If you must throw cold water on everything
then get a job as a fireman.

＄

Those who pride themselves on being hardboiled
are often only half-baked.

18

Give some people an inch
and they think they are rulers.

☙

Conceit is the only disease that makes everyone sick
except the one who has it.

☙

No man can push himself ahead very far
by patting himself on the back.

☙

The fellow who sings his own praise
often gets it in a key that's too high.

19

A good reply
to an atheist is to give him
an excellent dinner
and then ask if he believes
there is a cook.

He who stands high in his own estimation
is a long way from the top.

☙

The fellow with an inflated opinion of himself
is generally a "flat tire."

ॐ

Men wear their hair in 3 ways:
parted, unparted, and departed.

☙

The fellow that owns his own home is always
just coming out of the hardware store.

21

If your *walk* is not consistent with your *talk*,
you will frequently put your *foot* in your *mouth*.

Be like a good watch—have an open face,
busy hands, full of good works,
pure gold, and well regulated.

Others may doubt what you say,
but they will believe what you do.

It's not enough just to be good—
be good for something!

ℬ

When alone—guard your thoughts.
When at home—guard your temper.
When with friends—guard your tongue.

↭

The easiest thing to confess is—
my neighbor's sin.

Oftentimes the man
who most desperately needs help
is unwilling to admit he has a need.

The richest person
is the one who is contented
with what he has.

If you cannot get what you like,
why not try to like what you get?

Children are unpredictable.
You never know
what inconsistency
they're going to catch
you in next.

Contentment makes poor men rich;
Discontentment makes rich men poor.

Ꙅ

What counts most is not the size
of the dog in the fight,
it's the size of the fight in the dog.

Ꙅ

Next time a man tells you talk is cheap,
ask him if he knows how much
a session of Congress costs.

Congress is so strange.
A man gets up to speak and says nothing.
Nobody listens—
and then everybody disagrees.

ঌ

Many men who put antiknock in their automobiles,
ought to take a dose of it themselves.

ঌ

The man who rows the boat
generally doesn't have time to rock it.

Remember, when you point your finger
accusingly at someone else,
you have three fingers pointing at yourself.

🐦

When I start to find fault with all that I see,
it is time to start looking for what's wrong with me.

🐦

A good way to avoid heart trouble:
—don't run upstairs, and—
don't run down people.

28

Those who can see
God's hand in everything
can best leave everything
in God's hand.

The most loved folks in our community
seem to be the ones who never can recall
anything bad about any of us.

❧

A stateman is any politician it's considered safe
to name a school after.

☙

A political war is one in which everyone
shoots from the lip.

If you tell a man there are 300 billion stars
in the universe, he'll believe you.
But if you tell him a park bench has just been painted,
he has to touch it to be sure.

🦋

Some folks aren't interested in anything
unless it's none of their business.

🐚

Grandchildren are so much fun,
we should have them first.

31

When you are down in the mouth,
remember Jonah. He came out all right.

ᜍ

Don't despair because you have
occasional sinking spells of despondency
—just remember the sun has a sinking spell
every night.

🐝

If life gives you a lemon—
just make it into *lemonade*!

32

If you find a path with no obstacles
—it is probably a path
that doesn't lead anywhere.

❧

Of all sad words of tongue or pen,
the saddest are, "It might have been."

❧

Do not be discouraged—it may be the last key
in the bunch that opens the door.

33

His brother has a Ph.D.
His wife has an M.A.
His daughter has a B.A.
He is the only one
with a J.O.B.

If you go against the grain of God's laws,
you get splinters!

ॐ

Don't show off when driving.
If you want to race—go to Indianapolis!

☙

Always try to drive so that your license
will expire before you do.

ॐ

More people commit suicide with a knife, fork,
and spoon than with any other weapon.

35

It's not the *minutes* you spend at the table
than make you fat, it's the *seconds*.

໙

Did you ever notice
that people who don't count their calories,
usually have the figures to prove it?

ໜ

He who indulges bulges!

໙

Diets are for people who are
"thick and tired" of it.

36

Old accountants never die—
they just lose their balance.

ॐ

A chrysanthemum by any other name
would be a lot easier to spell.

ॐ

If you think education is expensive,
try ignorance.

ॐ

A hundred mistakes are an education
if you learn something from each one.

Don't be a *cloud*
because you failed
to become a *star*.

Most people are willing to pay more to be amused
than to be educated.

és

Oftentimes we don't appreciate life
until it's time for it to end.

↝

When two egotists meet,
it is a case of an "I" for an "I."

és

The man who knows *how* will find a job.
The man who knows *why* will be his boss.

39

He who climbs the highest
is he who helps another ascend.

The best thing to do behind a person's back—
is pat it!

People who are green with envy are ripe for trouble.

He who provides for this life,
but makes no provision for eternity,
is wise for a moment, but a fool forever.

We humans make provision for this life
as if it would never end, and we make provision
for the life to come as if it would never begin.

❧

We will have all eternity
in which to celebrate our victories,
but we have so little time left
in which to win them.

🌿

A man may make many mistakes,
but he is not a failure until he starts blaming
someone else for them.

41

Failures are divided into two categories:
—those who thought and never did, and—
those who did and never thought.

ðr

It takes thousands of nuts
to construct an automobile,
but only one nut
to scatter it all over the road.

·ð

Men who try something and fail are infinitely better
than those who try nothing and succeed.

Stand for something—
or you'll fall
for anything.

43

Abraham Lincoln declared you can't fool
all the people all the time, but highway
interchange signs come pretty close.

░

The world says, "Seeing is believing."
Faith says, "Believing is seeing!"

ↄ

Faith isn't believing in spite of evidence.
Faith is obeying in spite of consequence.

44

Feed your faith
and your doubts will starve to death.

ॐ

Faith is only as good as its object.
The man in the jungle bows before an idol of stone
and trusts it to help him,
but he receives no help.
If faith is not directed at the right object,
it will accomplish nothing.
The big question is, "In whom do you believe?"

The trouble with stretching the truth
is that it is liable to snap back.

⌁

The family that PRAYS together, STAYS together.
The family that TALKS together, WALKS together.
The family that SINGS together, CLINGS together.

🕊

God's children never say good-bye
for the last time.

If you want to set the world right,
start with yourself.

When looking for faults,
use a mirror, not a telescope!

If you are looking for an easy project—
try faultfinding. It requires no talent,
no brains, and no character to get started
in the business of grumbling.

47

Go as far as you can see.
When you get there,
you can see farther.

There are three ways we can get together:
First—We can be like popcorn in a popper and
explode at each other. Second—We can be like ice
cubes in a refrigerator and freeze together.
Third—We can be like a box of chocolates
in the summer sun and melt together.

ळ

If you think it doesn't pay to stick together,
consider the banana. As soon as it leaves the bunch
it gets skinned!

49

In our present condition, if someone offers you
the world on a silver platter—take the platter.

One of life's *hardest* jobs is to keep up
the *easy* payments.

A fish grows faster than anything living—
especially when a fisherman is describing it.

50

Many rejoice in being forgiven by God,
but they refuse to forgive others.

❧

Forgiveness is not condoning the wrong.

❧

Isn't it strange that men will fight for the right
to say what they think...and then say so much
without thinking?

It is true that a man is known
by the company he keeps.
It is also true that a man is known
by the company he keeps out of.

🐦

It is smart to pick your friends—but not to pieces.

🐦

A true friend is one who knows all about you,
and likes you just the same.

A true friend is one
who thinks you're a good egg
even though
you're half-cracked.

Platonic friendship: The interval between
the introduction and the first kiss.

❧

It's better to have a big heart than to own a big house.

❧

One thing the discovery of the North Pole revealed
is that there is nobody sitting on top of the world.

❧

When you have nothing left but God,
then for the first time you become aware
God is enough.

54

With God's strength *behind* you, his love *within* you,
and his arms *underneath* you, you are more
than sufficient for the days *ahead* of you.

❧

Little is much if God is in it.

❧

In the good old days, people quit spending
when they ran out of money.

❧

I wish people would give at least as much attention
to deeds as they do to creeds.

If you gossip and throw dirt, just remember,
you are losing ground.

ॐ

People who belong to the meddle class
have a keen sense of rumor.

ॐ

The truth of God's grace...humbles a man
without degrading him, and...exalts a man
without inflating him.

A husband who is a real diplomat always remembers his wife's birthday, but forgets what her age is.

ॐ

He who is thankful for *little* enjoys much.

ॐ

A sign of greatness is to be able to laugh at yourself with others—and enjoy it as much as they do.

ॐ

Great minds...discuss ideas. Average minds... discuss events. Small minds...discuss people.

57

If we could forget our troubles
as easily as we forget
our blessings, how different
things would be.

The man who is too big for a small job,
is too small for a big job.

It is greatness to do little things well.

Getting what they deserve
doesn't satisfy many people.

Dying is the last thing I ever intend to do.

59

When you feel dog-tired at night,
it may be because you growled all day.

When you need guidance, get close to God
and the nearer you are to him,
the clearer everything will appear.

Bad habits are like a comfortable bed...
easy to get into, but hard to get out of.

It's true that money talks, but in these days
a dollar doesn't have enough cents
to say anything worthwhile.

If you want to get rid of a pesty acquaintance
just lend him some money.

Two can live as cheaply as one...
and generally they have to.

It isn't your *position* that makes you happy
or unhappy, it's your *disposition*.

❧

Happiness is something that multiplies by division.

🐦

To find happiness, one must concern himself
with what he owes the world,
not with what the world owes him.

❧

It is not doing the thing we like that makes life happy;
it is learning to like the thing we have to do.

One reason why it's so hard
to save money is that our
neighbors are always buying
something we can't afford.

Some people cause happiness wherever they go;
others cause happiness *whenever* they go.

ↄ

Some folks sit and think, others just sit.

🌃

The parents of bright children
are strong believers in heredity.

ↄ

It is hard to make guests feel at home
when all the time you are wishing they were.

64

Many who expect to be saved
in the eleventh hour, die at ten-thirty.

❦

The easiest person to deceive is yourself.

❧

Live in such a way that the preacher
can tell the truth at your funeral.

❦

Some people are so heavenly minded
they are no earthly good.

65

Live the life, if you are going to talk the talk.

❧

One should give more concern to making a life
than to making a living.

❦

To rise to the top you must first
get to the bottom of things.

❧

One makes a living by what he gets;
he makes a life by what he gives.

66

It is when we forget ourselves
that we do things that will be
remembered.

Jumping to conclusions is not nearly so good
a mental exercise as digging for facts.

❧

Unless there is *within* us that which is *above* us,
we shall soon yield to that which is *about* us.

❧

Live each day as if it's your last—it may be.

❧

Nobody knows the age of the human race,
but all agree it is old enough to know better.

68

It takes more grace than one can tell
to play the second fiddle well.

ঙ্গ

The job many people spend most of their time at
—is the job of hiding what they really are.

৵

Some things come out better without our help...
like a bud opening into a beautiful flower.

Do you do your job each day well enough
that you would hire yourself?

ðª

A hearty laugh and a sunny smile combine
to produce the cheapest and best medicine
known anywhere in the world.

ðª

If you don't enjoy what you have now,
how can you be happier with more?

Show me a man getting an injection
from a cheerful nurse, and I'll show you a man
taking a friendly needling!

ঌ

If there is no sorrow for sin,
there will be no joy in salvation.

ﷺ

You are only as big
as the things that annoy you.

71

Remember—
even if you are
on the right track,
you'll get run over
if you just sit there!

You and I have no business setting ourselves up
as judges—unless we know all that God knows
about people.

ও

If you are *unkind*, you are the *wrong kind!*

ৡ

When it comes to giving,
some people stop at nothing.

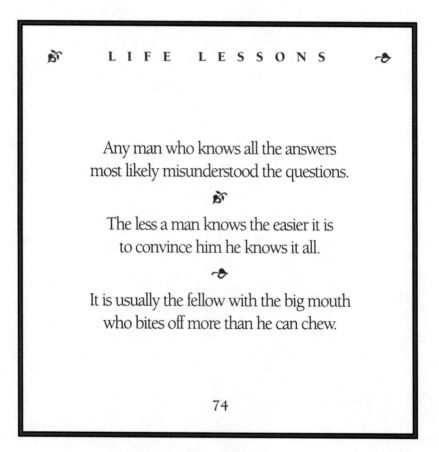

Any man who knows all the answers
most likely misunderstood the questions.

The less a man knows the easier it is
to convince him he knows it all.

It is usually the fellow with the big mouth
who bites off more than he can chew.

74

You can't leave your footprints on the sands of time
while sitting down.

❧

Sitting still and wishing makes no person great;
The good Lord sends the fishing
but you must dig the bait!

❧

Nothing is more exhausting than searching
for easy ways to make a living.

Many people are like a wheelbarrow—
they go no further than they are pushed.

He who continually watches the clock
need not worry about the future.
He simply doesn't have any.

Rip Van Winkle is the only person
who ever became famous while he was asleep.

76

We should learn something
every day.
Sometimes it is the discovery
that what we learned yesterday
was wrong.

If God has called you,
do not spend any time looking over your shoulder
to see who is following.

🐦

Some people suffer in silence—
much louder than others.

🐦

When life knocks you down to your knees
you are in a perfect position to pray.

It is easier to cope with out-and-out enemies
than with deceptive friends.

ॐ

Blessed is the man who has learned to admire
without envy, to follow without mimicking, to praise
without flattery, and to lead without manipulation.

↝

A valuable guideline for public speakers:
If you don't strike oil in 20 minutes, stop boring!

There are three rules for public speakers.
1. Stand to be seen.
2. Speak up to be heard.
3. Shut up to be appreciated.

❧

Advice to speakers: "Please keep in mind
that the mind cannot absorb more
than the seat can endure."

He who learns and learns but acts not what he knows,
is like one who plows and plows,
but never, never sows.

🐦

Sign seen in a kitchen: "The views expressed
by the husband are not necessarily
those of the management."

⤶

Signs seen in an office: "I'd like to compliment you
on your work. When will you start?"

81

If all else fails,
try following
directions.

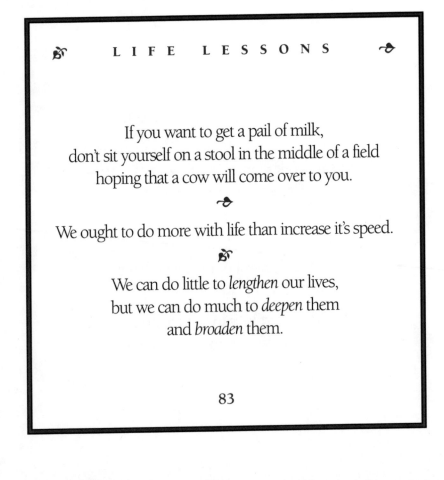

If you want to get a pail of milk,
don't sit yourself on a stool in the middle of a field
hoping that a cow will come over to you.

We ought to do more with life than increase it's speed.

We can do little to *lengthen* our lives,
but we can do much to *deepen* them
and *broaden* them.

83

If life is a grind—use it to sharpen your wits.

Be sure to work 8 hours—and sleep 8 hours—
but not the same 8 hours!

The difference between a luxury and a necessity is—
whether I have it or my friend has it.

The worst lie is to lie to myself.
The worst deceit is to deceive myself.

84

A lie is a coward's way of getting out of trouble.

Your income tax reveals two things:
the amount of your income,
and the amount of your honesty.

Those who tell white lies soon become color blind.

I can keep a secret but the folks I tell it to can't.

The cause of broken marriages is selfishness
in one form or another.

How disappointing when they say,
"I didn't know you'd been away."

A lesson in mathematics:
A little sin will...*add* to your trouble;
subtract from your energy;
and *multiply* your difficulties.

You can never
be quite sure
what kind of mind
a person has
until he gives you
a piece of it.

Few men ever grow up—
they merely change their toys.

❧

Some people conduct their lives
on the cafeteria plan—self-service only.

❧

Middle age is the time when a narrow waist
and a broad mind change places.

Vacant lots and vacant minds usually become
dumping grounds for a lot of rubbish.

ॐ

Many minds are like concrete—
all mixed up and permanently set.

ॐ

A great many so-called "open minds"
should be closed for repairs.

Refuse to engage in a battle of wits
with anyone who is unarmed.

To love the whole world for me is no chore.
My tough problem's the neighbor next door.

The greatest of all faults is to imagine you have none.

Things could be worse—suppose your errors were
published every day like those of baseball players?

90

Most of us would get along well
if we used the advice we give others.

ঙ

A man is always as young as he feels,
but seldom as important.

ঙ

Men and pins are useless
when they lose their heads.

Learn from the mistakes
of others.
You won't live long enough
to make them all
yourself.

92

To err is common and normal.
To admit it is very unlikely.

A mistake, if understood,
is but a step toward wisdom.

If money is all you want,
money is absolutely all you'll get.

The hardest kind of money to get is—enough.

It is unfortunate to have more dollars than sense.

☙

It isn't what you have in your pocket
that makes you thankful,
but what you have in your heart.

☙

It's tough to be poor...
but not as bad as being in debt.

☙

The real measure of a man's worth is--how much
would he be worth if he lost all his money?

94

When your *outgo* exceeds you *income*,
your *upkeep* causes your *downfall*.

ɞ

The reason a young man leaves the farm
to work in the city is to make enough money
to retire and move back on the farm.

ɞ

A fool and his money are soon invited places.

ɞ

Nothing is *all* wrong. Even a clock
that has stopped running is right twice a day.

95

A man who says he is doing as much at 60
as he did at 20, wasn't doing much at 20.

࿐

An ounce of mother is worth a pound of preacher.

࿐

Nothing is more frequently "opened by mistake"
than the mouth.

࿐

Old age can't seem to catch up with folks who have
more things to do than they can possibly finish.

96

Great opportunities
come to those
who make the most
of the small ones.

You never get a second chance
to make a good first impression.

🐚

When opportunity knocks,
some people object to the noise!

⤳

There is only one endeavor
in which you can start at the top
and that's digging a hole!

The Lord has given us two ends,
they have a common link;
For with the bottom end we sit,
and with the other we think.
Success in life depends upon
which end you choose to use.
You'll soon discover this my friend,
Heads you win and *tails* you lose!

Much more important than adding years to your life,
is to add life to your years.

❧

They can't call you an old dog
as long as you are learning new tricks.

❧

The best thing about growing old
is that it takes such a long time.

❧

Hardening of the heart ages people more quickly
than hardening of the arteries.

An optimist defines a window
as something to let the light shine through.
A pessimist defines a window
as something that gets dirty and needs washing.

When the outlook is bad,
try the *up-look*.

All work and no play makes Jack a dull boy—
and Jill a wealthy widow.

101

Prayer is
asking for rain.
Faith is carrying
the umbrella.

102

One of the greatest labor-saving inventions
of today is tomorrow.

ὅ

Oftentimes when we hear our children talk,
we realize we should have been more careful
of what they heard us say.

☙

The best inheritance a parent can give his children is
—a few minutes of his time each day.

Bring up a child in the way he should go,
and go that way yourself.

🐦

Don't let your parents down—
remember, they brought you up.

🐦

Parents can tell but never teach,
Until they practice what they preach.

🐦

Be a patient pedestrian—
otherwise you'll be a pedestrian patient!

An old proverb declares,
"Dwell on the past and you'll lose an eye;
forget the past and you'll lose both eyes."

❧

It is always too soon to quit.

❧

People don't plan to fail--they just fail to plan.

❧

A good thing to remember, and a better thing to do;
is to work with the construction gang
and not the wrecking crew.

105

A pint of example is worth a gallon of advice.

To praise God for our miseries—ends them.
To praise God for our blessings—extends them.

You will not stumble while on your knees.

Nothing lies beyond the reach of prayer
except that which lies outside the will of God.

The will of God
will never lead you
where the grace of God
cannot keep you.

It is as natural for the spiritual man to pray
as it is for the natural man to breathe.

⤚

The prayer of a Sioux Indian:
"Great Spirit, help me never to judge another
until I have walked two weeks in his moccasins."

🐚

God will not accept praying as a substitute for obeying.

⤚

People who do a lot of kneeling
don't do much lying.

Do not face the day
until you have faced God.

❧

It is never too late to give up your prejudices.

❧

I will study and get ready, and maybe my chance
will come. (Abraham Lincoln)

❧

There's not much sense
keeping your nose to the grindstone
just to turn it up at the neighbors.

The bigger a man's head gets,
the easier it is to fill his shoes.

ॐ

It is too bad people can't exchange problems
with each other, for all of us claim we know
how to solve the other fellow's problem.

ॐ

The best way to forget your own problem
is to help someone else solve his.

110

The trouble with being punctual
is that nine times out of ten there is nobody
there to appreciate it.

The person who uses the loudest voice
is the one who has the weakest argument.

Let's learn the lesson that we "can disagree
without being disagreeable."

111

If revenge is sweet,
why does it leave
such a bitter taste?

The only thing worse than a quitter
is the man who is afraid to begin.

🐦

A quitter never wins and a winner never quits.

⤴

Be sure you're wrong before you quit.

🐦

If you are not living as close to God as you once did,
you need not guess who moved.

To look around--is to be distressed. To look within—is to be depressed. To look to God—is to be blessed.

❧

The man who puts God *first*
will find God with him right up to the *last*.

❧

When God measures a man, he puts a tape
around his heart—not his head!

❧

If God is your partner...make your plans BIG.

114

God is *for* us—that is good.
God is *with* us—that is better.
God is *in* us—that is best.

The secrets of the Lord are for those
who live close to him.

The fellow who's on his toes
doesn't usually have any trouble
keeping other people
from stepping on them.

Men with clenched fists cannot shake hands.

See what you can do for others;
not just what *they* can do for you.

When you try to make an impression—
that is precisely the impression you make.

While seeking happiness for others
we unconsciously find it for ourselves.

Try to be satisfied
with your lot,
even if you don't
have a lot.

To handle yourself...use your head.
To handle others...use your heart.

৵

To return evil for good is..devilish;
To return good for good is...neighborly;
To return good for evil is...godlike.

ॐ

Don't worry about what people
think about you—the chances are
they seldom think about you at all.

118

He who lives for God's honor and glory
seeks neither praise nor reward, but in the end
he is certain of both.

The crowd is usually going the wrong way.
Sacred and secular history indicate that it is usually
God's righteous minority bucking the crowd
that is going the right way.

The way of least resistance usually goes downhill.

119

A rumor is like a check—don't endorse it
until you are sure it's genuine.

෨

Beware of a half-truth—
you may have gotten the wrong half.

෬

How lamentable is the way we praise
the dead saints and persecute the living ones!

120

The devil's number one strategy
is to get you to procrastinate.

ॐ

Fortune smiles upon the person
who can laugh at himself.

❧

If you could kick in the pants
the fellow responsible for most of your troubles,
you wouldn't be able to sit down for six weeks.

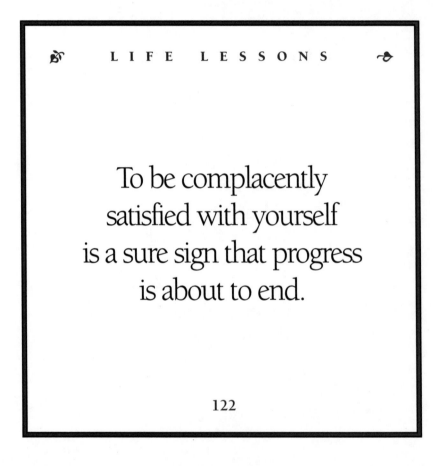

To be complacently
satisfied with yourself
is a sure sign that progress
is about to end.

Whatever you may be sure of, be sure of this—
you are dreadfully similar to other people.

⤙

We ask God to provide for our needs,
and when he does, we congratulate ourselves
on our ability and cleverness.

🌸

A man wrapped up in himself
makes a very small package.

123

There is hope for any man who can look in the mirror
and laugh at what he has seen.

ॐ

Everyone can do something to make the world
better—he can at least improve himself.

◆

Sinful pleasures can make you laugh,
but they can never dry your tears.

ॐ

The trouble with a little sin is that it won't stay little.

Sin produces a moment of gratification
and an eternity of remorse.

If you don't want the fruits of sin,
stay out of the devil's orchard!

Smiles never go up in price or down in value.

It has been said that a smile
adds a lot to your face value.

125

We'll be in trouble as long as we pay the best
professors less than the worst football coach.

The average person hasn't stored up
enough treasure in heaven to make
a down payment on a harp.

Be like a postage stamp—it sticks to one thing
until it gets the job done!

The smartest person is not the one
who is quickest to *see through* a thing,
rather it is the person who will *see a thing through*.

❦

If you want to get a true estimate of a man,
observe what he does when he has nothing to do.

❧

Most of us would rather be ruined by flattery
than to be benefitted by criticism.

Remember, success
comes in "cans,"
failure comes in "can'ts."

A valuable measure of success or failure
is whether the tough problem you are facing
is the same problem you had a year ago.

There are many roads to success—
but they are all uphill.

If at first you don't succeed—
you are about average.

Those who never succeed themselves
are always first to tell you how.

It's no fun to suffer in silence unless you first make
enough noise to attract attention and sympathizers.

It is rather ridiculous to think we are better
than Grandpa and Grandma simply because
we have better and shinier gadgets.

It seems a little silly now, but this country
was founded on a protest against high taxes.

No one wants to listen to you talk,
unless he believes it will be his turn next.

He who thinketh by the inch,
and talketh by the yard,
ought to be dealt with by the foot!

131

There is a vast difference between having to say something and having something to say.

We must never be silent when we ought to speak.
We must never speak when we ought to be silent.

As a man grows wiser, he talks less and says more.

The trouble with a fellow who talks too fast is that he is apt to say things he hasn't even thought of yet.

132

God gave us two ears
and only one mouth,
which indicates we should
listen twice as much
as we talk.

If you must speak your mind,
then mind how you speak.

🐦

Before you give somebody a piece of your mind,
be sure you can get by with what you have left!

🐦

You can't get rid of your temper by losing it.

🐦

When you are right, you can afford
to keep your temper. When you are wrong,
you can't afford to lose it.

134

If you can't convince 'em, confuse 'em.

↪

When you flee temptation, be sure
you don't leave a forwarding address.

Ӿ

The words "think" and "thank"
come from the same Latin root.

↪

If we take the time to *think* more
we will undoubtedly *thank* more.

135

You cannot stop people from thinking...
the job is to get some people started.

ᴥ

When you stop to think,
don't forget to start again.

ᴥ

You can do better than you think.
You can do better if you think.
You can do better—don't you think?

136

If you must kill time,
why not try to work it to death?

ঌ

The test of tolerance comes when we are in a majority.
The test of courage comes when we are in a minority.

ঔ

Tomorrow is the busiest day of the week.

ঌ

The best preparation for tomorrow
is the right use of today.

137

Yesterday is gone;
Tomorrow is uncertain;
Today is here.
So *use* it!

Tomorrow isn't likely to be much fun for the fellow
who couldn't find anything to enjoy today.

🐦

The only bit that will bridle the tongue
is a little bit of love.

🐦

A sharp tongue is no indication of a keen mind.

🐦

Let's learn a lesson from tea.
It shows its real worth when it gets into hot water.

139

There are very few gains without pains...
and very few triumphs without trials.
There is no sunshine without shadows.

We are God's jewels. Often God exhibits
his jewels on a dark background...
so they will shine more brightly.

Be confident of this—if God sends you on stony paths,
he will provide you with strong shoes.

The brook would lose its song
if you removed the rocks and stones.

⤴

God's love does not always keep us *from* trials,
but it is a love that always keeps us *through* trials.

※

There can be no victories without battles.
There can be no peaks without valleys.
There can be no roses without thorns.

There is only one person who likes to hear
about your troubles—your lawyer.
He gets paid for it!

☙

Trust him—when dark days assail you;
Trust him—when your faith is small.
Trust him—when to simply trust him
is the hardest thing of all.

❧

Never be afraid to trust an unknown future
to a known God.

142

Do it *now*! Today will be yesterday tomorrow.

Sadder than work left unfinished
is work never begun.

There are two kinds of people
who never amount to much:
those who can't do what they are told,
and those who can do nothing else.

The only people with whom you should try
to get even are those who have helped you.

❧

The more a man is addicted to vice,
the less he cares for advice.

❧

When a man becomes wealthy
the important question is: "Will God gain a fortune
or lose a man?"

Truth needs
no crutches.
If it limps,
it's a lie!

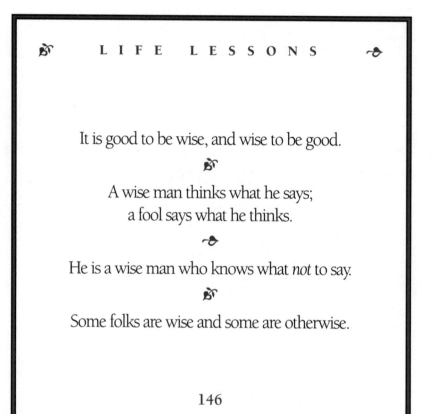

It is good to be wise, and wise to be good.

A wise man thinks what he says;
a fool says what he thinks.

He is a wise man who knows what *not* to say.

Some folks are wise and some are otherwise.

The brain is no stronger than its weakest *think*.

↝

The greatest undeveloped territory in all the world
lies under your hat.

ℬ

A woman's work is never done—
especially if she asks her husband to do it.

↝

You should never criticize your wife's judgment—
look who she decided to marry!

A painting in a museum hears more ridiculous
opinions than anything else in the world.

❧

Don't be afraid of opposition—
a kite rises against the wind, not with it.

❦

Sharp words will upset the stomach,
especially if you have to eat them.

Many people avoid discovering the secret
of success because deep down they suspect
the secret may be—*hard work!*

🐦

After all is said and done,
there is much more said than done.

↝

The quickest way to get a multitude
of things accomplished is to do
just "one thing at a time."

149

If your method is "hit or miss"
you will usually miss.

🐦

It is better to say, "This one thing I do,"
than to say, "These forty things I dabble in."

🐦

For heaven's sake—what on earth are you doing?

🐦

Plan your work—then *work your plan*.

If a thing will go
without saying—
then let it go!

Every tomorrow has two handles.
We may take hold of it by the handle of anxiety,
or we can take hold of it by the handle of faith.

ᥱ

There is a great difference
between *worry* and *concern*.
Worry frets about a problem.
Concern solves the problem.

152

Faith ends where worry begins,
and worry ends where faith begins.

❧

There are 773,692 words in the Bible,
but not once can we find the word "worry"
among them. The conclusion is obvious—
if "worry" is not in God's vocabulary,
it should not be in ours.

Worry is an emotion that can never empty
tomorrow of its problems, but it does empty today
of its strength. It does not help us escape evil,
but it does make us ill-prepared to cope
with it when and if it comes.

⤙

Defeat can be the beginning of success
...a colt is not much good until he's been broken.
Neither are we.

Don't fret and worry about the future.
Do what you know you ought to do today.
The rest is God's responsibility.
He has promised to be with us
each step of the way.
What more can we ask for?

Do unto others
as though you were
the others.